D1526726

Women and Sports

A YOUNG WOMAN'S GUIDE
TO CONTEMPORARY ISSUES™

Women and Sports

LAURA LA BELLA

ROSEN
PUBLISHING®

New York

Published in 2013 by The Rosen Publishing Group, Inc.
29 East 21st Street, New York, NY 10010

Library of Congress Cataloging-in-Publication Data

La Bella, Laura
Women and sports/Laura La Bella. — 1st ed.
      p. cm. — (A young woman's guide to contemporary issues)
Includes bibliographical references and index.
ISBN 978-1-4488-8398-1 (library binding)
1. Sports for women—Juvenile literature. I. Title.
GV709.L3 2013
796.082—dc23

                                                            2012012016

Manufactured in the United States of America

CPSIA Compliance Information: Batch #W13YA: For further information, contact Rosen Publishing, New York, New York, at
1-800-237-9932.

Contents

INTRODUCTION

Olympic gymnast Shawn Johnson. Soccer goalie Hope Solo. NASCAR driver Danica Patrick. Olympic Alpine skier Lindsey Vonn. Grand Slam tennis aces Venus and Serena Williams. Golf star Michelle Wie. These are some of the biggest names in the world of women's sports. They are household names. They compete internationally in their respective sports. They earn millions of dollars for their athletic

ability and are sought after by companies worldwide for endorsement deals.

But not long ago, as early as the 1950s, seeing female athletes compete at the highest levels of sport was unheard of. Athletics were a purely male-centered endeavor. For centuries, sports were an arena where boys and men proved their physical strength and power, and women were relegated to the sidelines as spectators. As women pushed for the right to participate in sports, they faced discouragement, discrimination, and mistreatment. Even after federal legislation legally called for equality for women in athletics, female athletes still had to fight for their right to play. While much has changed, female athletes still fight to overcome a number of issues, despite the successes of

athletes like Johnson, Solo, Patrick, Vonn, Wie, and the Williams sisters.

As much success as these top female athletes have accomplished, a dark side exists to women's sports. Judged equally by their athletic ability and their appearance,

HOPE SOLO, THE GOALIE FOR THE U.S. WOMEN'S NATIONAL TEAM, DIVES TO SAVE A BALL. DURING THE 2011 WORLD CUP, SOLO WAS AWARDED THE BRONZE BALL, AN HONOR BESTOWED ON THE TOURNAMENT'S THIRD-BEST PLAYER.

female athletes face pressures their male counterparts do not. The pressure to be thin, attractive, and feminine while also being strong and athletic is so great that eating disorders have become a serious matter in many female-dominated sports. Body image issues, eating disorders, and steroid use are commonplace for athletes in sports such as gymnastics and figure skating, where appearance is considered as important as athletic ability.

Many female athletes face expectations to be strong and skilled competitors while also exhibiting femininity. For those who seem to appear less stereotypically feminine, questions about their sexuality often overshadow their athletic abilities. Topping it off are society's views of female athletes and the images of women saturating the media. Female athletes are featured on magazine covers and in advertisements as being feminine, sexy, or overly styled as opposed to their male counterparts, whose athletic abilities and strength are highlighted. How the media covers women's sports illustrates the importance the media has in shaping society's view of female athletes and its acceptance of women as equal to men in the sports world.

For the female athlete who can conquer all of these obstacles, she will still be hit head-on with a staggering inequity in pay compared to male athletes. Tennis star Maria Sharapova was the highest-paid female athlete in 2011, earning a staggering $25 million. That same year, professional golfer Tiger Woods earned $75 million, triple what Sharapova made. In fact, the ten highest-paid female athletes made a total of $113 million in 2011, while the ten highest-paid male athletes made a collective $449 million.

For all the progress women have made in academia, the workplace, politics, and government, the false specter of female frailty still casts a dark shadow over women in sports. For example, some female sports feature shorter playing times, or women are given certain advantages to make up for perceived handicaps (e.g., a smaller ball, a closer starting point). True equality of opportunity and competition on the sports field is still elusive for female athletes.

There are thousands of female athletes who have shattered expectations and risen to the top of their sport, but issues of equality, competition, gender expectations, and other barriers still affect female athletes from high school and college to professional sports.

CHAPTER 1

A History of Women in Sports

In 776 BCE, the first Olympic Games were held in ancient Greece. Women were not only excluded from competition, they weren't even allowed to watch the men compete. In protest, women organized their own sporting competition, called the Games of Hera. They competed every four years in honor of the Greek goddess Hera, who ruled over women.

Fast forward to the modern Olympic Games, where every two years the world watches as some of the most powerful female athletes gather to compete in events as diverse as swimming, skiing, figure skating, gymnastics, ice hockey, speed skating, soccer, cycling, weight lifting, and track and field. On display are feats of outstanding athletic skill, endurance, strength, agility, and speed. Much has changed for women at the Olympics and for female athletes everywhere.

IMPORTANT MOMENTS IN WOMEN'S OLYMPIC HISTORY

- Women first compete at the 1900 Paris games in lawn tennis and golf.
- In 1912, women began competing in swimming events, but not American women, who were not allowed to compete in any event that did not allow them to wear long skirts.
- In 1976, gymnast Nadia Comaneci scored a perfect 10 seven times.
- American Joan Benoit Samuelson won the first women's Olympic marathon in Los Angeles in 1984. That same year women were first allowed to compete in cycling.
- Women's hockey was accepted as a full-medal sport at the 1998 games in Nagano, Japan. The U.S. women's team won the gold medal.
- The 2000 Olympics was the first time that women were allowed to compete in weight lifting.

A RIGHT TO PLAY

Women have been excelling at athletics for centuries. In the 1550s, Mary, Queen of Scots, was known as an avid golfer. In 1858, Julia Archibald Holmes climbed Pikes Peak in Colorado. Women's college basketball and baseball teams date back to the 1860s. Then, many of these activities were more recreational than competitive. At the time, it was believed that women should not, and could not, exert themselves physically.

MEMBERS OF THE LOS ANGELES JUNIOR COLLEGE ARCHERY TEAM GET ONE FINAL PRACTICE SESSION IN BEFORE THE NATIONAL INTER-COLLEGIATE ARCHERY TOURNAMENT IN 1935. AT THE TIME, ARCHERY WAS ONE OF ONLY A FEW SPORTS IN WHICH WOMEN COULD PARTICIPATE.

But women knew better. As they continued to insist on their right to play sports, women's club and intermural teams cropped up at colleges all over the country. It wasn't until the women's suffrage movement in the late nineteenth and early twentieth centuries, which saw the passing of the

Nineteenth Amendment that gave women the right to vote, that women felt empowered to pursue other freedoms. This included their equal right to compete in athletics.

At first, women's engagement in sports was limited. Sweating, physical contact, and competition were not "ladylike" behaviors, so opportunities for women to be athletic were constricted to sports like golf, archery, and croquet. These activities were among the first sports considered acceptable for women because they were not strenuous, nor did they involve physical contact.

The pursuit of women's equality in sports took a big leap forward during World War II. In the 1940s, many men entered the military to fight in the war, leaving women behind to fill their positions in factories and in the workplace. This gave women the opportunity to prove they were equal to men in the workforce and could handle working outside the home while managing their roles as homemakers. These new roles also gave women the self-esteem and confidence to push for full equal rights.

The war not only gave women entry into the workforce, it also gave them a starring role in the first women's professional baseball league. At the time, with so many young men being drafted for the war, Major League Baseball was canceled. Baseball league executives were looking for a way to keep the sport in the public eye while its male stars were away fighting the war. Philip K. Wrigley, owner of the Wrigley chewing-gum company and the Chicago Cubs, gathered other baseball executives and started a new professional league with women players.

In 1943, the All-American Girls Professional Baseball League was created. The league, which had its story featured in the 1992 Hollywood film *A League of Their Own*, was popular with fans. Wrigley emphasized the importance of being feminine and projecting the image of

A *League of Their Own* is a 1992 film that offers a fictionalized account of the development of the All-American Girls Professional Baseball League.

SICAL Women Athletes FEMALE STEROIDS
EOTYPING SPORTS Equal Rights PERFECTION EQUALITY

"the All-American Girl Next Door," all while featuring players with outstanding athletic ability. The league included fifteen teams, and each season culminated with a league championship. The league stayed in operation until 1954.

After World War II ended, and still riding the popularity of the women's baseball league, organizations for women in sports began to increase. Women's athletics became more competitive, and intercollegiate and interscholastic competition spread. This movement would eventually lead to the passing of Title IX, federal legislation that would help to equalize the opportunities for and treatment of women in athletics.

SEPARATE BUT STILL NOT EQUAL

Even though Title IX helped to level the playing field between men and women in sports, the struggle for recognition and equality continues to this day. A survey of 303 Division I schools, conducted by USA Today, found that since 1992, the number of women college athletes has increased by 22 percent. However, the survey also revealed that for every $1 spent on women's college sports, $3 is spent on men's. Women receive only 38 percent of scholarship funds and only 27 percent of recruiting funds.

Even the structure of organized athletics today, from youth leagues to the Olympics, supports a belief that women can't play as long or as hard as men. The false assumption that women are inferior to men has led to a sharp gender division in sports. For example, in tennis

KALANA GREENE (#32) OF THE UNIVERSITY OF
CONNECTICUT HUSKIES DRIVES PAST JAYNE APPEL (#2) OF
THE STANFORD UNIVERSITY CARDINALS DURING THE NCAA
WOMEN'S FINAL FOUR SEMIFINALS. THE HUSKIES BEAT THE
CARDINALS AND WENT ON TO BECOME THE NCAA
NATIONAL CHAMPIONS.

SICAL Women ATHLETES FEMALE STEROIDS
SPORTS Equal Rights PERFECTION EQUALITY

matches, women play three games while men play five. In golf, women start closer to the hole than men do, and in youth leagues girls play nine holes while boys play the full eighteen. These notions suggest that men's sports are to be taken more seriously than women's sports and that women don't have the power, stamina, or ability to compete equally with men.

While physical differences do exist between men and women, they should not dictate rules for endurance. Instead, these physical differences should inspire a different set of rules only for those sports in which extremely physical contact occurs, such as football or boxing, where the physical strength of male and female athletes is not equal and could lead to an unfair advantage or injury if coed play were allowed. But in sports where such physical power has little if any influence, specific gender-based rules are unnecessary.

Coed adult sports leagues are the perfect example of how these gender rules are senseless and unnecessary. In some coed basketball leagues, women earn two points for every basket while men earn only one. Coed softball leagues are known to enforce rules such as having no more than two men bat in a row. Sometimes men are pitched larger balls while women are pitched smaller ones. These rules assume that men are better athletes than women or that women need to be given an advantage because they don't have the ability to play by a more demanding and rigorous set of rules.

The University of Connecticut's women's basketball team would argue that a separate and less stringent set of rules is not needed for women to prove their dominance in a sporting event. From 2008 to 2010, the Huskies won ninety games in a row, breaking the previous record streak of eighty-eight games set by the 1970s-era UCLA men's team. During this time, the Huskies also won two back-to-back NCAA national championships. In basketball, the court isn't smaller for women, the quarters of play aren't shorter, and the points awarded for baskets are the same.

Ten Great Questions
TO ASK AN ACADEMIC ADVISER

1.
What are the academic performance requirements to remain a student-athlete?

2.
What is the graduation rate among student-athletes?

3.
What kinds of athletic scholarships are available?

4.
What is required of me to maintain my athletic scholarship?

5.
What happens to my scholarship if I'm injured and unable to participate in my sport?

6.
How much time per week is required for practice?

7.
Will I have access to academic support, such as tutors, to help me with my studies if I fall behind?

8.
How much travel is involved for my sport?

9.
If I miss a class, assignment, or exam because I am traveling for a sports competition, what is the policy for making up missed work?

10.
How demanding are the academic programs?

CHAPTER 2

Gender Roles in Sports

University of New Mexico women's soccer defender Elizabeth Lambert was suspended indefinitely in 2009 after multiple infractions during a game against Brigham Young University. Throughout the game, Lambert elbowed, kicked, and punched players from the opposing team. At one point, she yanked a Brigham Young player to the ground by her ponytail. Is this fearless competition, overly aggressive play, or poor sportsmanship?

Division I soccer is a physical contact sport, for both men's and women's teams. In men's soccer, we see forceful, sometimes hostile physical performances, but none seem to gain the media attention that Lambert's actions did. Could it be that we don't expect a pretty, young female athlete to act in a violent, aggressive manner?

What happens when female athletes are too good or play aggressively like male athletes? Society has a difficult time accepting women as formidable, assertive athletes.

Play Like a Girl

If Elizabeth Lambert had been a male player, it's likely that none of her actions would have resulted in the footage of the soccer game going viral on the Internet or in Lambert being assaulted verbally and threatened in blogs and in e-mail messages, as she was. But Lambert is far from the first female athlete to exhibit confrontational actions during a sporting event. In fact, these types of actions aren't uncommon in women's sports. Lambert's behavior illustrates a continuing challenge female athletes face: when being competitive, is there a place for traditional notions of femininity in sports?

In 2008, eleven WNBA players were suspended after a shoving match between the Los Angeles Sparks and the Detroit

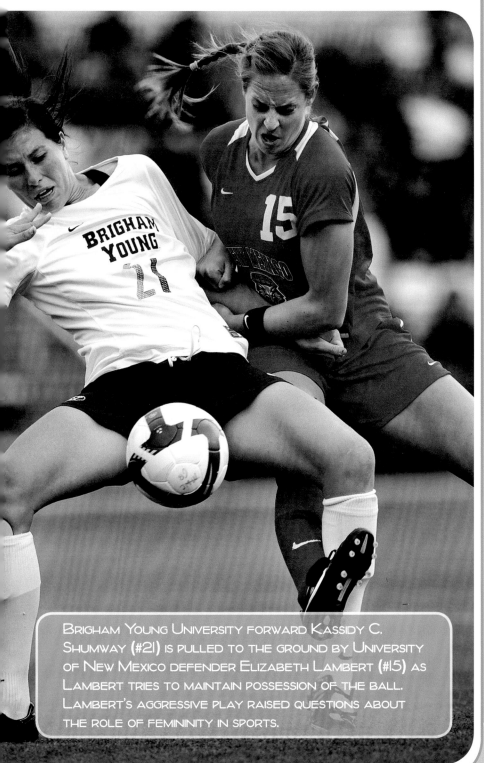

BRIGHAM YOUNG UNIVERSITY FORWARD KASSIDY C.
SHUMWAY (#21) IS PULLED TO THE GROUND BY UNIVERSITY
OF NEW MEXICO DEFENDER ELIZABETH LAMBERT (#15) AS
LAMBERT TRIES TO MAINTAIN POSSESSION OF THE BALL.
LAMBERT'S AGGRESSIVE PLAY RAISED QUESTIONS ABOUT
THE ROLE OF FEMININITY IN SPORTS.

Shock. That same year, Serena Williams verbally assaulted and threatened a U.S. Open line judge after she disagreed with a call. Both of these incidents attracted national attention. Yet, we see examples of physical confrontation regularly in men's sports, from fistfights in hockey games and trash talking on the basketball court of an NBA game to a bounty system rewarding violent hits that knock opposing players out of a football game in the NFL. Society rarely questions when a male player acts inappropriately, but when a female athlete does, it is labeled unladylike and the athlete is called emotionally unbalanced, hysterical, irrational, or unnatural. When female athletes demonstrate characteristics that go against what society deems as

"ladylike" behavior, traditional gender roles are challenged.

Gender roles are a set of social behaviors that are considered to be appropriate for individuals of a specific

BOXERS ARELY MUCINO OF MEXICO AND MELISSA McMORROW OF THE UNITED STATES, BOTH RANKED AMONG THE TOP TEN FLYWEIGHTS IN THE WORLD, FIGHT FOR THE WBA WOMEN'S INTERIM FLYWEIGHT WORLD TITLE.

sex. Traditional gender roles expect men to be rational, strong, hardworking, and masculine, while women are to be domestic, nurturing, feminine, and emotional. Gender roles are often used to tell people how they are supposed to act and look, and even what one's interests should be. Little girls are given dolls and play kitchens as toys, while little boys receive trucks and sporting equipment.

Athletes in particular are often evaluated and judged by the very narrow and confining criteria of traditional gender roles. Women and girls who excel in sports challenge society's perception of the way women and girls are supposed to act and what they are supposed to be interested in. When we see an athlete like Lambert acting physically, aggressively, or even violently on a playing field, it goes against how society expects a woman to behave. Although it has become somewhat more acceptable for female athletes to participate in traditionally male-dominated sports, like hockey, wrestling, or boxing, there is a lingering negative connotation attached to those female athletes who attempt to do so. When women exhibit what society considers more manly traits, they face questions about their gender identity, sexual orientation, values, and social roles.

THE IMAGE OF THE FEMALE ATHLETE

For female athletes who participate in sports that require skills that are typically considered "male characteristics," such as speed and strength, an image problem can arise. Society does not know how to view or portray these female athletes.

When the U.S. women's soccer team won the World Cup, *People* magazine featured a story about the team. Very few action shots from the soccer tournament were used. Instead, the magazine featured photos of the players with their husbands, boyfriends, and children. Research has shown that by featuring female athletes in more traditional gender roles—in this case, as wives, girlfriends, or mothers—they become more acceptable to the public. In many cases, female athletes must prove they live their lives off the field according to traditional gender roles. For female athletes who either appear more masculine or exhibit exceptional athletic ability, questions about their sexual orientation often arise. Many female athletes face questions or insinuations that they are gay. Media coverage of men's sports focuses on their athletic accomplishments, while female athletes' personal and domestic lives are included in profiles of their athletic successes.

Abby Wambach was the 2011 Associated Press Athlete of the Year. She is a star of the women's U.S. World Cup soccer team and is among soccer's top five highest goal scorers. She's one of the most decorated female soccer players of all time and one of the world's most recognizable soccer players. When she began garnering international attention for her outstanding soccer abilities, questions started circulating about her sexual identity. Instead of focusing on skill and talent, there is an effort placed on wanting to understand or explain why the athlete differs so greatly from traditional standards of femininity.

THE TEN MOST INFLUENTIAL FEMALE ATHLETES OF ALL TIME

1. **Babe Zaharias:** The first great female athlete became a national superstar. Zaharias gained national attention during the 1932 Olympics Games, where she won gold medals in the javelin and 80-meter hurdles and a silver medal in the high jump. Three years later, she entered women's professional golf. She would end up winning forty-one golf tournaments, including ten major wins. She also competed in three men's golf tournaments, becoming the first woman to qualify for a men's golf event.

2. **Jackie Joyner-Kersee:** Joyner-Kersee is often regarded as the greatest female athlete of the last century. She dominated the 1984, 1988, 1992, and 1996 Olympic Games, winning three gold medals, one silver medal, and two bronze medals in the women's heptathlon and women's long jump. She was also a champion at multiple World Championships and Pan American Games.

3. **Martina Navratilova:** Navratilova's long career in tennis resulted in eighteen Grand Slam singles titles, thirty-one Grand Slam doubles titles, and ten Grand Slam mixed doubles titles. She also holds the record for the most singles and doubles titles.

4. **Mia Hamm:** Women's soccer and Mia Hamm go hand in hand. With 158 international goals, she has scored more goals than any other soccer player, male or female. She led the U.S. women's team to two Olympic gold medals and two FIFA World Cup championships.

5. **Steffi Graf:** For almost seven years, Graf was the number one ranked women's tennis player in the world. She won twenty-two Grand Slam singles titles, the second-most all-time victories among both female and male tennis players, and 107 singles titles overall, the

third-most among women. In 1988, Graf won all four major tournaments and a gold medal at the Olympic Games. She is the only tennis player in history to accomplish this feat.

Annika Sorenstam: As the most successful female golfer ever, Sorenstam won ten major golf championships, gained seventy-two tour wins, and earned more than $22 million during her fifteen-year career. Because of her success, she was invited to play in the men's Bank of America Colonial golf tournament in 2003, where she became the first woman to compete in a men's tour event since Babe Zaharias.

Billie Jean King: King famously defeated male tennis great Bobby Riggs in "the Battle of the Sexes" in 1973, proving that a female tennis player could compete at the highest levels of the sport and even against some of the sport's leading male players. The outcome of the match was especially important because it occurred during a time when there still wasn't equality for women in sports. By the end of her career, King earned twelve Grand Slam singles titles, sixteen Grand Slam doubles titles, and eleven Grand Slam mixed doubles titles.

Bonnie Blair: Blair is the most decorated female U.S. winter Olympian of all time, having won five gold medals and one bronze medal in speed skating in the 1988, 1992, and 1994 Olympic Games. She was inducted into the U.S. Olympic Hall of Fame.

Florence Griffith-Joyner: Known as "Flo-Jo," Griffith-Joyner still holds the world records in the 100 meters and 200 meters, which she set in 1988. At the 1984 Los Angeles Olympic Games, Griffith-Joyner won a silver medal, and in the 1988 Seoul Games she won three gold medals.

10. **Nadia Comaneci:** As the first gymnast to score a perfect ten in an Olympic event, Comaneci had a successful career as a gymnast. She won five gold medals and became one of the best-known gymnasts in the world.

STEREOTYPING FEMALE ATHLETES

Alaina Sudeith was always a tomboy, and her classmates at the University of California at Los Angeles knew and accepted this about her. But the moment she joined the water polo team, her peers suddenly had a different view of her. Many now assumed she was gay.

Many female athletes competing in those sports commonly viewed as being "masculine," such as boxing, ice hockey, and soccer, or those that have wrongly been associated with primarily lesbian participation, such as softball and basketball, find they must conform to traditional stereotypes associated with women to avoid having their sexual identity questioned and examined. Many female athletes, to avoid being mislabeled or having assumptions made about them, will manage their appearance so that they look more stereotypically feminine. They will wear skirts and high heels, put on makeup, and style their hair to fight the perception that they are gay. This form of discrimination is called heterosexism.

Heterosexism is a form of discrimination that favors people who are straight over those who are gay. It affects women regardless of their actual sexual orientation. Many gay athletes are hesitant to come out publicly for fear that they will be discriminated against or lose the support of fans, teammates, coaches, and sponsors. Athletes who are straight, but whose sexuality may be questioned because of their athletic ability or the assumptions made about their sport, often overcompensate and try to appear "hyper-feminine" in an effort to dispel any doubt about their sexual identity.

MARTINA NAVRATILOVA

Martina Navratilova won eighteen Grand Slam titles over the course of her tennis career, including six consecutive Wimbledon championships, and was ranked number one for 331 weeks. She became the first female athlete to earn more than a million dollars in a year. But throughout her early career she faced questions about her sexuality. In 1981, at the height of her success, Navratilova ended the speculation by coming out, even after being advised not to by tennis officials who were afraid she would lose corporate sponsorships. Even though Navratilova's honesty did indeed cost her millions of dollars in endorsement opportunities, she went on to became one of the greatest tennis players in the world, an activist for gay rights, and a positive role model for other gay athletes who face a hard decision about whether to speak publicly about their personal lives.

MARTINA NAVRATILOVA IS ONE OF THE GREATEST FEMALE ATHLETES OF ALL TIME. SHE WON EIGHTEEN GRAND SLAM TITLES DURING HER CAREER AND BECAME A ROLE MODEL FOR GAY ATHLETES IN 1981 WHEN SHE CAME OUT AT THE HEIGHT OF HER CAREER.

Embracing Their Assets

Some female athletes fight the media's gender-stereotyped coverage of them. They argue that, by portraying female athletes either as sexy or beautiful, the media is spreading a message that says women are not as skilled, strong, powerful, or capable as male athletes. Other female athletes, however, embrace the way the media covers them and use it to their advantage. They are challenging the assumption that sexy images undermine the importance and validity of women's athletics. These athletes are savvy about marketing and understand how creating and managing their own images can bring more attention to their athletic abilities and increase their overall popularity.

GoDaddy.com—a company that registers Internet domain names—is a sponsor of Danica Patrick's racing team. Patrick is the first female driver to win an IndyCar race. In television ads for GoDaddy, she appears in a bikini wearing four-inch heels. Patrick doesn't shy away from using her appearance to garner attention, nor does she apologize for it. She uses the fact that she's an attractive woman to her advantage. Patrick told the *New York Times*, "I'm a girl, and so to say I can't use being a girl doesn't make any sense. In this world, there's so much competition out

DANICA PATRICK, THE FIRST FEMALE DRIVER TO WIN AN INDYCAR RACE, HAS EMBRACED THE ATTENTION SHE GETS FOR HER ATTRACTIVE APPEARANCE. SHE HAS USED THE MEDIA TO HER ADVANTAGE AND, AS A RESULT, IS AMONG THE WORLD'S MOST RECOGNIZABLE ATHLETES.

there that you have to use everything that you have to make sponsors happy, to attract them, to be unique, to be different."

Patrick has embraced what makes her unique in a sport dominated by men. She knows how to market herself and has used the media to her advantage. As a result she is one of the most recognizable names in racing. According to Nielsen/E-Poll N-Score, which tracks the public's awareness of individual athletes, 30 percent of the population knows who Patrick is. The average male race car driver is known by only 9 percent of the population, as are most female athletes. Patrick has also brought more attention and viewers to her sport. In 2011, there was a 17 percent higher television viewing audience for the twelve races she participated in.

Women's professional golf is not known for the sex appeal of its players. Natalie Gulbis, who has won three major tournaments, is challenging that notion. She is a rising star in women's professional golf and is capitalizing on both her skills and her appearance to raise awareness of her performance and of women's golf in general. Gulbis has participated in the *Sports Illustrated* swimsuit issue, regularly appears on covers of national magazines, and is well known for producing an annual swimsuit calendar. She even has her own reality series on the Golf Channel, which features a behind-the-scenes look at her life on and off the golf course.

Patrick's and Gulbis's acceptance of the ways in which media covers women's sports, and their skill at taking advantage of society's need to view women as attractive and feminine, raises an important question: why do women have to choose between being athletic and being beautiful or feminine? Does a sexy image of a female athlete have to be inherently demeaning? Women should not have to choose between being athletic and being feminine. They can embrace their athletic accomplishments and celebrate their femininity without feeling as if doing so is personally degrading or in some way damaging to women's athletics as a whole.

Patrick, Gulbis, and other athletes, such as gymnast Alicia Sacramone, tennis player Caroline Wozniacki, and Olympic swimmer Natalie Coughlin, have all actively participated in photo shoots and marketing campaigns that flaunt their beauty. This approach, as Patrick and Gulbis have proved, can attract more attention to a female competitor and her strictly athletic accomplishments.

CHAPTER 3

EQUAL RIGHTS IN ATHLETICS

At sixteen years of age, Wilma Rudolph qualified for the 1956 Olympics where she won a bronze medal in the 4x100-meter relay. Four years later, at the Rome Olympic Games, Rudolph would became the first American woman to win three gold medals in track and field during a single Olympics. Rudolph became a nationally beloved athlete, garnering attention as a successful female athlete during a time in history when women's athletics were known for being noncompetitive physical activities instead of feats of skill, strength, and speed.

The Olympic Games were one of the few venues where female athletes competed against one another. While women have always participated in sports and sporting events, organized competitive athletics didn't become a reality in the United States until the passing of federal legislation that would require equality for female athletes.

WILMA RUDOLPH WON THREE GOLD MEDALS AT THE 1960 OLYMPIC GAMES. HER SUCCESS HELPED TO CHANGE THE PERCEPTION OF WOMEN IN ATHLETICS.

TITLE IX CHANGED EVERYTHING

The passing of the Civil Rights Act of 1964, which was written to end discrimination based on race, color, or national origin, energized women to push for more gender equality and better defined women's rights. Congress-woman Patsy Mink, who wrote the legislation for Title IX, originally focused on the hiring and employment practices of federally financed institutions. Her goal was to ensure that women were treated equally to men in all hiring practices.

While Title IX doesn't mention sports specifically in its legislation, it does provide overriding protection from discrimination based on sex in educational programs and activities that receive money from the federal government. Title IX ensures that:

- Women and men are given equal opportunities to participate in sports

- Female and male student-athletes receive athletic scholarship dollars proportional to their participation in sports

- Female and male student-athletes are provided for equally when it comes to sporting equipment; scheduling of

games and practices times; travel; coaching; athletic, training, and housing facilities; medical and training staff; support services; and recruiting

When President Richard Nixon signed the act on July 23, 1972, only about thirty-one thousand women were involved in college sports at the time. Less than $100,000

PATSY T. MINK, A CONGRESSWOMAN FROM HAWAII, WROTE THE LEGISLATION FOR TITLE IX, WHICH ENSURED THAT WOMEN WERE TREATED FAIRLY IN EDUCATIONAL PROGRAMS AND ACTIVITIES THAT RECEIVED FUNDING BY THE FEDERAL GOVERNMENT.

was spent on athletic scholarships for women, and colleges had less than half the number of women's teams as they did men's teams.

Several organizations fought against the mandates of Title IX, including the National Collegiate Athletic Association (NCAA), which tried to block the legislation in the 1970s and 1980s. Some colleges cut men's athletic programs in order to comply with Title IX. Several male athletes sued over program cuts, and some female athletes were blamed for the colleges' decisions. A key argument made against Title IX was that it appeared to inspire gender discrimination against men.

As recently as 2000, President George W. Bush called for a reexamination of Title IX. He issued revised guidelines that inserted loopholes in the legislation that made it easier for colleges and universities to avoid their obligation to provide equal opportunities to female athletes. President Barack Obama reversed Bush's weakening of Title IX and fully restored the original legislation. After considerable lobbying by women's groups, laws were put in place to punish those who did not comply with Title IX.

FAR-REACHING BENEFITS OF TITLE IX

Just six years after Title IX was passed, the percentage of girls playing team sports jumped from 4 percent to 25 percent. In 1972, close to thirty thousand women were competing in NCAA-sponsored sports. Today, there are more than 160,000 female student-athletes competing in college sports. The impact of Title IX reaches far beyond sports. The increase in girls' athletic participation was associated with a 7 percent lower risk of obesity twenty to twenty-five years later, when this first generation of Title IX girls were women in their late thirties and early forties.

There are incredible benefits to playing sports for girls. In addition to making friends, having fun, and learning new skills like teamwork and leadership, athletics impact girls' lives in valuable ways:

- **Empowerment:** Female athletes are more confident and have better self-esteem. They also have a more positive body image than those who don't play sports.

- **Better Grades:** Being involved in sports helps girls do better in school. Exercise helps to improve memory and concentration, which helps students learn more effectively. Sports also require students to manage their time. Those involved in a number of activities, including sports, tend to be more efficient with time management and juggling schedules.

- **Teamwork and Goal-Setting Skills:** Learning to be a team player is an important lesson. Later in life, when women get jobs, they will work with a variety of different personalities. Learning to work together to solve problems and meet goals is essential for success both on and off the field. Playing sports also reinforces math and leadership skills.

- **Health Benefits:** In addition to being fit and maintaining a healthy weight, athletes are less likely to smoke, have a lower risk of getting certain cancers, including breast cancer, and have reduced incidence of other illnesses, such as osteoporosis, later in life. Girls who are athletic often are at a healthier weight and have a reduced risk of becoming obese. They have better blood pressure and blood sugar levels and lower cholesterol.

- **Manage Stress and Pressure:** It can be stressful to manage your studies, a part-time job, family commitments, and friendships. Sports help to diffuse stress and give you an outlet to work off anxiety and pressure. Physical activity is a natural mood lifter and helps to fight depression. Having teammates who share the same experience can also help you feel like you have a built-in support group that understands what you are going through.

- **General Wellness:** Girls who play sports report feeling happier than those who don't participate in athletics. They often have more energy and enjoy a better overall quality of life.

THE TEN HIGHEST-PAID FEMALE ATHLETES

1. **Maria Sharapova (tennis)**, $25 million: Her recent eight-year, $70 million endorsement deal with Nike is one of the biggest in sports.

2. **Caroline Wozniacki (tennis)**, $12.5 million: For sixty-seven weeks she held the number one ranking in women's tennis.

3. **Danica Patrick (NASCAR/Indy)**, $12 million: Patrick is the only woman to ever win an IndyCar series race. Her third-place finish at the 2009 Indianapolis 500 was the highest finish by a woman in the event's history.

4. **Venus Williams (tennis)**, $11.5 million: With twenty-one Grand Slam titles and three Olympic Gold medals, Williams is one of the most decorated women in tennis.

5. **Kim Clijsters (tennis)**, $11 million: A former number one ranked tennis player, Clijsters retired from play in 2007, but returned in 2009. In only her third tournament after returning to the game, she won her second U.S. Open title.

6. **Serena Williams (tennis)**, $10.5 million: With twenty-seven Grand Slam titles, Williams is one of only five women to ever hold all four Grand Slam titles at the same time.

7. **Kim Yu-Na (figure skating)**, $10 million: The 2010 Olympic Gold medalist, Kim is the most recognizable athlete in her native South Korea.

8. **Li Na (tennis)**, $8 million: Li became the first Chinese player to win a singles Glam Slam event when she won the 2011 French Open.

9. **Ana Ivanovic (tennis)**, $6 million: Ranked seventeenth in the world, Ivanovic signed a lifetime endorsement deal with Adidas that makes her one of the top earners in women's tennis.

10. **Paula Creamer (golf)**, $5.5 million: The 2010 U.S. Women's Open champion, Creamer has won eleven tournaments.

COMPETING ON AN EQUAL FOOTING WITH MEN

Title IX tried to provide equality for women's sports in high schools and colleges, but the federal legislation did not

PHYSICAL Women ATHLETES FEMALE STERO
STEREOTYPING SPORTS Equal Rights PERFECTION EQU

impact sporting events held outside of the confines of academic institutions. Women still had to fight for participation in a number of sporting events not sponsored by or organized under the auspices of academia.

In 1967, Kathrine Switzer became the first woman to

officially register and compete in the Boston Marathon. She did so under false pretenses. At the time, women were not allowed to race in the Boston Marathon, so Switzer registered under "K. Switzer." While running, Switzer was nearly forced off the course by Jock Semple, a race official who tried to tear off her race number and physically remove her from competition. Switzer's then-boyfriend blocked Semple, and Switzer finished the race. Switzer's extraordinary effort sparked an interest in women's running. She continued to compete in races, winning the 1974 New York City Marathon.

JOCK SEMPLE TRIES TO PULL KATHRINE SWITZER (#261) FROM THE COURSE OF THE 1967 BOSTON MARATHON BUT IS BLOCKED BY SWITZER'S THEN BOYFRIEND. SWITZER COMPLETED THE RACE AND BECAME THE FIRST WOMAN TO FINISH THE BOSTON MARATHON.

Switzer has dedicated her career to creating opportunities and equal sport status for women. She created the Avon International Running Circuit, a series of international running events for women in more than twenty-five countries. Her support and advocacy for women's running led to the inclusion of the women's marathon in the Olympic Games.

No Equality in Pay

While Title IX has helped to level the playing field for women as regards participation in athletics, it hasn't helped to equalize the earnings or salaries of professional female athletes and coaches with those of their male counterparts. Prize money is much less for women than men in nearly all sports. Take professional golf. The total prize money for the PGA tour, $256 million, is more than five times that of the LPGA tour, which is $50 million. For a WNBA player with a minimum of three years in the league, the minimum salary is $54,000. For NBA players, the minimum salary for a first-year player is more than $473,000.

Very few sporting events award equal prize money to men and women. For finishing in third place in the 2003 Women's World Cup, each U.S. women's national soccer team member was awarded $25,000. They would have

ABBY WAMBACH, A FORWARD FOR THE U.S. WOMEN'S NATIONAL TEAM, AND HER TEAMMATES EARNED $25,000 EACH FOR FINISHING THIRD IN THE 2003 WORLD CUP. BY COMPARISON, THE MEMBERS OF THE U.S. MEN'S NATIONAL TEAM EARNED $200,000 EACH FOR REACHING THE QUARTERFINALS.

received $58,000 if they had won the World Cup. Just for reaching the quarterfinal of the World Cup in 2002, the U.S. men's national soccer team members received $200,000 each. In 2007, Wimbledon announced for the first time that the tournament would award equal prize purses to male and female tennis players. All four Grand Slam events now offer equal prize money to the champions.

The pay inequity trickles down to coaches as well. Female head coaches of Division I teams received an average salary of $850,400, while head coaches for men's teams average $1,783,100.

CHAPTER 4

THE PRICE OF PERFECTION

In the 1980s, Christy Henrich was an up-and-coming gymnastics star. A top U.S. gymnast, Henrich took fifth place in the all-around at the national junior championships. She was only thirteen years old at the time. She later finished tenth at the senior nationals, a tournament considered a stepping-stone to the Olympics. But after a meet, Henrich received some negative feedback during a critique session with a U.S. judge, who suggested she was "too fat" to make the Olympic team.

Devastated by the comment, Henrich focused on losing weight while she trained for the Olympics. She weighed just 90 pounds (41 kilograms) when she competed for a spot on the 1988 Olympic team. But she would miss making the cut by a heartbreaking 0.118 of a point on the vault.

Henrich developed an eating disorder, anorexia nervosa, a condition in which one severely limits the amount of calories consumed. Henrich once commented that she

U.S. GYMNAST CHRISTY HENRICH (SHOWN WITH HER FIANCÉ, BO MORENO) WEIGHED ONLY 60 POUNDS (27 KG) WHEN SHE DIED FROM MULTIPLE ORGAN FAILURE AFTER A LONG BATTLE WITH EATING DISORDERS.

PHYSICAL Women ATHLETES FEMALE STE
STEREOTYPING SPORTS Equal Rights PERFECTION

could survive on just three apples a day. Henrich's illness took such a toll that she was forced to retire from gymnastics after repeated hospitalizations. At twenty-two years old, Henrich died from multiple organ failure. She weighed only 47 pounds (21 kg) at the time of her death.

Henrich took extreme measures in her attempt to attain her goals. Yet it's not uncommon for female athletes to have disturbed eating patterns, develop full-blown eating disorders, or take steroids to control their appearance or enhance their performance.

Dying to Win

Gymnast Cathy Rigby was instructed by her coaches not to weigh more than 85 pounds (39 kg). The gymnast, who in the 1960s and 1970s won twelve international medals over the course of her career, suffered from bulimia for years. Twice Rigby almost died after suffering from cardiac arrest due to an electrolyte imbalance caused by her eating disorder. Even after retiring, Rigby continued to battle bulimia.

According to two studies of college athletes conducted by eating disorder experts, at least one-third of all female athletes exhibit some level of disordered eating. This can range from constant dieting and taking laxatives and diet pills to the occasional binge eating and purging. Some athletes become so obsessive about their weight that they develop serious eating disorders, like anorexia nervosa or bulimia nervosa.

For female athletes, athletic ability and appearance are judged hand in hand. Because of this added emphasis on physical beauty, rather than just physical ability, eating disorders are a common and serious issue among female athletes. Certain sports, such as gymnastics, diving, dance, and figure skating, where there is a judging system that is subjective, put pressure on an athlete to be not only athletic and powerful, but also to be thin and pretty. This is true even though one's looks have no effect on one's physical performance.

Seven-time Olympic gold medalist Amanda Beard has struggled with an eating disorder since she was a teenager. At the 1996 Olympics, at just fourteen years old, Beard became the second-youngest Olympic medalist in American swimming history when she won three gold and two silver medals. The next year, a normal growth spurt added 8 inches (20 cm) and 25 pounds (11 kg) to Beard's body. After performing poorly at a swim invitational, Beard read newspaper articles predicting the demise of her career and calling her Olympic victories a fluke. Beard began struggling with body issues and developed an eating disorder. At its worst, she would force herself to throw up six to seven times a day.

OLYMPIC GOLD MEDALIST AMANDA BEARD HAS SPOKEN PUBLICLY ABOUT HER STRUGGLE WITH BODY IMAGE AND EATING DISORDERS. ACCORDING TO RECENT STUDIES, NEARLY ONE-THIRD OF FEMALE ATHLETES STRUGGLE WITH EATING DISORDERS.

Henrich's and Beard's stories are common for women in sports. Women athletes experience an immense pressure to be thin and to maintain a certain body weight or shape. The prevalence of eating disorders among female athletes competing in sports in which aesthetics are important—such as figure skating and gymnastics—is significantly higher than female athletes who participate in nonaesthetic or non-weight-dependent sports, such as weight lifting, soccer, or volleyball.

Henrich's eating disorder, anorexia nervosa, is characterized by an obsessive fear of gaining weight. People with anorexia nervosa feel hungry but deny themselves full meals. Instead, they allow themselves to eat only very small amounts of food. Anorexia nervosa is a serious mental illness. It can lead to hair loss, depression, a distorted self-image, bad breath, general poor health, malnutrition, and heart disease. In extreme cases, like Henrich's, death can result from organ failure due to starvation.

Beard's disorder, bulimia nervosa, is an illness in which a person binge eats, or eats excessive amounts of food, then purges the food she just ate by forcing herself to vomit. Bulimia sufferers also abuse laxatives, use diuretics, or engage in excessive exercise. Bulimia nervosa is nine times more likely to occur in women than men. It can lead to serious health issues such as infertility, chronic gastric reflux, constipation, and an electrolyte imbalance, which can lead to cardiac arrhythmia, cardiac arrest, and even death.

SIGNS AND SYMPTOMS OF AN EATING DISORDER

Athletes with eating disorders often go to great lengths to conceal their condition. Many will wear loose clothing, refuse to eat with others, and isolate themselves. The following signs and symptoms indicate an eating disorder may be developing in a young athlete.

- Restrictive dieting
- Purging through vomiting, diuretics, or laxatives
- Withdrawal from teammates
- Chronic fatigue
- Excessive exercise outside of set practice or training times
- Inability to complete workouts
- Avoiding dressing/undressing in front of teammates
- Avoiding eating in front of others
- Weight loss
- Loss of concentration
- Dehydration
- Pale, dry skin
- Hyperactivity
- Gastrointestinal problems
- Frequent use of restrooms
- Cold intolerance
- Changes in mood
- Isolation
- Depression
- Fainting
- Light-headedness
- Decreased stamina

NADIA COMANECI, A NINE-TIME OLYMPIC GOLD MEDALIST AND ONE OF THE MOST FAMOUS FACES IN WOMEN'S GYMNASTICS, STRUGGLED WITH EATING DISORDERS AND THE PRESSURE TO LOOK A CERTAIN WAY.

When Food Becomes the Enemy

A healthy athlete knows that food is fuel for her body. Muscles need protein, and carbohydrates give an athlete the energy to compete hard. However, an athlete with a distorted view of food and eating doesn't see food as a source of energy and fuel. Instead, she views food simply in terms of unwanted calories and fat.

Eating disorders are found in all sports and can afflict men as well as women. But for athletes participating in activities that emphasize a thin, slender body for optimal performance, such as figure skating, gymnastics, and swimming, the risk for developing an eating disorder is significantly greater. A cross-country runner might seek to control her weight by eating less. She thinks this will make her lighter and faster. A gymnast might want to lose weight because she thinks judges are looking at her size and shape as well as her ability. She believes that being thinner might improve her scores.

Obsessively counting calories and restricting food intake wreaks havoc on an athlete's body and will affect her performance. The body needs food for energy as well as muscle growth and regeneration. Without energy and nutrients, the body can't perform as well, endurance suffers, and muscle strength and the immune system weaken.

Even the biggest names in women's athletics are not free of the pressure to achieve a particular look. Nadia Comaneci, the nine-time Olympic gold medalist in gymnastics, admitted to suffering from both anorexia and bulimia. Nancy Kerrigan, a two-time Olympic medalist in figure

MARIAN JONES, WHO WAS STRIPPED OF HER OLYMPIC MEDALS, LEAVES COURT AFTER BEING SENTENCED TO SIX MONTHS IN JAIL FOR LYING TO INVESTIGATORS ABOUT HER INVOLVEMENT IN USING PERFORMANCE-ENHANCING SUBSTANCES.

PHYSICAL Women ATHLETES FEMALE STERO STEREOTYPING SPORTS Equal Rights PERFECTION

skating, has also struggled with an eating disorder.

ATHLETES AND STEROIDS

Marian Jones was at one time considered to be one of the greatest female athletes in history. She was the fastest female runner in the world, with world records in the 100-meter and 200-meter events. Her successful quest to become the first female athlete to win five medals in track and field in one Olympics at the 2000 Sydney games was followed by news organizations and awestruck viewers around the world.

A year after her historic Olympic performance, however, Jones was suspected of using performance-enhancing drugs. It would take six more years before Jones would admit to using steroids, which she told investigators she began using in 1999. Jones was stripped of her Olympic medals and sent to prison for six months after pleading guilty to lying to investigators about her use of steroids. It was a sad end to a career that was watched by millions of people around the world and, in particular, by young girls everywhere who were inspired by Jones to become athletes themselves.

Steroid use by athletes is a dark secret in sports. Steroids are synthetic hormones that help the body to produce muscle and help muscles recover faster from tough workouts. They can lessen or prevent muscle breakdown and increase the level of testosterone in the body. Testosterone is a hormone that stimulates muscle tissue to grow bigger and stronger. Some steroid medications are legal, but these are available only with a doctor's prescription. Obtaining them in any other way is against the law.

Athletes use steroids for a number of reasons. Steroids can help muscles become more defined and stronger. They can boost self-esteem and confidence. They can help athletes perform more effectively. Steroids can also reduce the recovery time that muscles require after workouts or competition. But steroids are unhealthy and even dangerous. For women, the side effects can be drastic. Female athletes who take steroids can experience a deepening of their voice, hair loss, aggressive behavior, mood swings, and depression. They lose the natural curves that are typically associated with a woman's body, and their breasts can shrink in size. Many women will see their bodies become more masculine looking.

Steroid use has extremely negative repercussions for the body, and these harmful effects can last for years, even long after consumption stops. The liver and heart can be damaged permanently. In addition, reproductive disorders and other illnesses, such as diabetes, can occur later in life as a result of steroid abuse, long after an athlete is no longer competitive.

Aside from the physical impact that steroids have on a woman's body, steroids are illegal. For athletes found using them, the penalties are steep. Professional and college athletes are regularly drug tested. A woman who fails a drug test can be kicked off her team and forced to forfeit any awards or trophies she has earned. She can also face serious legal actions, fines, and even jail time.

TEENS AND STEROID USE

Steroids aren't found just in the locker rooms of professional athletes. They are also present in high schools and colleges and are used by teens as young as thirteen to help influence their athletic performance. A study in 2008 surveyed students in grades eight through twelve. Of those who admitted using steroids, 57 percent said steroid use among professional athletes influenced their decision. Eighty percent of these teen steroid users said they believed steroids could help them achieve their athletic dreams and that they were willing to take the risks associated with steroid use if it meant they could reach the professional level of competition.

Even though teens know the physical harm that steroids can cause, many still don't see anything wrong with using them. Even though a number of athletes in recent years have been involved in steroid scandals—from more than eighty Major League Baseball stars to players on the North

Nutrition Facts
Valeur nutritive
Per 32 g serving (1 scoop)
par portion de 32 g (1 cuillère)

	% Daily Value
Amount Teneur	% valeur quotidienne
Calories / Calories 120	2 %
Fat / Lipides 1	1 %
Saturated / saturés 0.2 g	
+Trans / trans 0 g	
Polyunsaturated / polyinsaturés 0.1 g	
Monounsaturated / monoinsaturés 0.5 g	0 %
Cholesterol / Cholestérol 0 mg	13 %
Sodium / Sodium 310 mg	7 %
Potassium 230 mg	0 %
Carbohydrate / Glucides 1 g	0 %
Dietary Fibre 0 g	
Sugars / Sucres 0 g	
Protein / Protéines 27 g	0 %
Vitamin A / Vitamine A	0 %
Vitamin C / Vitamine C	10 %
Calcium / Calcium	25 %
Iron / Fer	

Other Ingredients / Autres ingrédients :
Sucralose   10 mg

SERVINGS PER CONTAINER : 18
PORTIONS PAR CONTENANT : 18

Amino Acid Analysis (per 32 g)
Analyse des Acides Aminés (par 32 g)

Alanine
Arginine
Aspartic acid / acide aspartique
Cysteine / cysteine
Glutamic acid / acide glutamique
Glycine
*Histidine
*Isoleucine
*Leucine
*Lysine
*Methionine / methionine
*Phenylalanine / phenylanine
Proline
Serine / serine
Threonine
*Tryptophan
Tyrosine
*Valine

STEROID USE IS ON THE RISE AMONG HIGH SCHOOL AND COLLEGE ATHLETES. PERFORMANCE-ENHANCING DRUGS CAN HAVE SERIOUS AND DANGEROUS EFFECTS ON THE BODY.

Korean women's World Cup soccer team—most teens still believe it should be a professional athlete's right to use steroids if he or she chooses.

While steroids are illegal, there are a number of performance-enhancing supplements, such as protein powders, creatine, and amino acids, that can be used to build body mass. Other supplements, such as pills that encourage the burning of fat, high-energy drinks, ephedra, and caffeine pills, are used to control weight. While legal, none of these supplements are healthy, and abuse of them is dangerous.

CHAPTER 5

SOCIETY, CULTURE, WOMEN, AND SPORTS

Lindsey Vonn is a highly decorated alpine skier. She won a gold medal at the Vancouver Winter Olympics and has won fifty-two World Cup races—third on the all-time women's list. Since 2008, she has won two World Championship golds, four World Cup overall crystal globes, five straight World Cup season titles in downhill, and three straight in combined. In 2010, the U.S. Olympic Committee named Vonn its Sportswoman of the Year.

Media coverage followed her success at the Olympics, including the cover of *Sports Illustrated*. Yet instead of featuring an action shot of Vonn skiing down a mountain, emphasizing her athletic talent, the magazine portrayed Vonn in a suggestive position on its cover. This was yet another example of how female athletes are significantly more likely to be portrayed in ways that emphasize their femininity and heterosexuality rather than their athletic prowess.

Magazine covers of female athletes, like U.S. skier Lindsey Vonn, typically focus more on appearance than physical ability. Media portrayal of female athletes often encourages society to take women's sports less seriously than men's sports.

SICAL Women Athletes FEMALE STEROIDS
SOLOTYPING SPORTS Equal Rights PERFECTION EQUAL

Tennis star Roger Federer has won a record sixteen Grand Slam singles titles. On a cover of *Sports Illustrated*, a photo of Federer highlights his power and strength as he stands ready to strike a tennis ball. Anna Kournikova, one of the best-known female tennis players in the world, was also featured on a cover of *Sports Illustrated*. She, however, was portrayed first and foremost as an attractive, sexy woman instead of a powerful athlete. Kournikova was photographed with her long blond hair down and styled, wearing a pink blouse, and lying on a pillow.

MEDIA PORTRAYAL OF FEMALE ATHLETES

Men's sports and male athletes are predominately featured on sports networks like ESPN, in advertisements for products, and on magazine covers in ways that emphasize their athletic ability and achievements. In contrast, female athletes are portrayed as sexy instead of athletic and powerful. Study after study has revealed that newspaper and television coverage around the globe routinely focuses on the purely athletic exploits of male competitors while offering hypersexualized images of their female counterparts. Media images that focus on femininity or sexuality disrespect female athletes and place a greater—and highly irrelevant—emphasis on looks rather than athletic ability.

Even among female athletes, looks, not athletic ability, seem to count for more. Tennis player Mary Pierce has won four Grand Slam titles. Fellow tennis star Anna Kournikova has never won a major tournament. During a recent Wimbledon tournament, Kournikova was hailed as

ANNA KOURNIKOVA, A TENNIS PLAYER WHO HAS NEVER WON A MAJOR TOURNAMENT, GETS MORE ATTENTION DUE TO HER APPEARANCE THAN OTHER TENNIS PLAYERS WHO HAVE WON MAJOR TOURNAMENTS AND ARE NATIONALLY RANKED.

one of the best role models for women's tennis, despite her having never won a major title and with champion players such as Pierce and the Williams sisters competing at Wimbledon that year. Kournikova, who is judged to be more feminine than the sportier and more skilled and successful Pierce, is even seen as a more "acceptable" athlete by tennis representatives.

WHAT'S ON TELEVISION? NOT WOMEN'S SPORTS

Every five years, since 1989, a study is conducted that analyzes the amount and type of coverage women's sports receive by sports media outlets such as ESPN. Researchers found that less than 2 percent of sports coverage was devoted to women's sports. They also found that the type of coverage women's sports received was less about outstanding play, individual achievements, or team accomplishments and more about specific incidents in women's sports, such as hair pulling during a soccer

game. The study's results support an argument media scholars have been making for years: a consequence of the media's tendency to present female athletes as sexy and attractive, focusing less on their athletic ability and accomplishments, reinforces the idea that women's sports are second-rate and therefore not worthy of being as respected as men's sports.

EACH YEAR THE WOMEN'S COLLEGE NCAA MARCH MADNESS BASKETBALL TOURNAMENT HAS RECORD ATTENDANCE AND HIGH TV RATINGS, WHICH CHALLENGES THE NOTION THAT WOMEN'S SPORTS FAIL TO FIND AN AUDIENCE.

♀ PROFESSIONAL WOMEN'S SPORTS: A CONSTANT STRUGGLE

The U.S. women's professional soccer league suspended operations for the 2012 season, citing poor attendance at games. This came only one year after the U.S. Women's National soccer team made it to the finals of the World Cup. Lack of fan interest—among both male and female spectators and viewers—makes it a struggle to launch and maintain professional women's sports leagues.

While boys who played baseball often grow up to be men who watch baseball, the same is not true of girls. Studies have shown that women do not consume sports in the same way men do. Super Bowl XLVI in 2012 drew an audience of 43.3 million women. It was the highest-rated Super Bowl in terms of female viewership, but that doesn't mean that all those women are football fans. The fact that the Super Bowl tends to inspire social gatherings, parties, and group viewership helps to explain why the number of women watching the game is so high.

Poor viewership among women of women's sports has led to a lack of success by women's professional sports leagues. The WNBA, a professional women's basketball league, has enjoyed some success, yet it is completely underwritten by the NBA. It would probably not survive if it relied solely on viewer interest and ticket buyers and the advertising revenue that goes along with them.

It's not that women's sports fail to find an audience. Each year during the NCAA's March Madness tournament, women's college basketball games have record attendance and high TV ratings. Coverage highlights the long-standing traditions of some of the college teams, conference rivals, and legendary coaches. Women's World Cup soccer also consistently receives strong TV ratings. The 2011 World Cup final between the United States and Japan was the second-highest-rated soccer game ever watched on American television. Both these events showcase strong, athletic women exhibiting great skill in their respective sports.

But those responsible for promoting women's sports, mainly journalists, marketing professionals, and advertisers, take a different approach. They see the depiction of female athletes as feminine and attractive as the best strategy for selling women's sports to a mainly male television audience.

Female athletes claim national and world titles in a number of sports and win gold, silver, and bronze medals at the Olympics year after year. But more and more, media images of female athletes cast them in overly feminine roles or hypersexualized roles. For example, a profile of professional golfer Donna Andrews featured a photo of her in an evening gown. U.S. soccer player Brandi Chastain was pictured in *Gear* magazine with no visible clothing on, but holding two soccer balls in front of her. Images of female athletes tend to be either nonthreatening to men (Andrews in an evening gown) or overly sexualized (Chastain wearing very little). Studies show that men see high-performing women as a threat to the traditional male dominance of sports.

SPORTS AND LATINA ATHLETES

National studies show that Hispanic girls have some of the lowest percentages of participation in sports. Unique cultural influences often influence their interest in and ability

Lisa Fernandez, a pitcher for the U.S. national softball team, is one of very few Latina athletes. An emphasis on education to the exclusion of extracurriculars has contributed to the low numbers of Latina athletes.

to take part in athletics. In Latino culture, families often have old-fashioned views concerning the proper roles of men and women. Traditionally, Latina girls often help out with family obligations after school, whether watching younger siblings or pitching in around the house with chores or preparing dinner while their parents are working. These responsibilities leave little time for sports or make it hard for a girl to make a commitment to a sports team when she can't be at practice on a regular basis.

Sports are also not seen as a priority in many Latino families. Social pressures and ethnic and cultural traditions often shape girls' attitudes about femininity, competition, and aggression. These attitudes can sometimes serve to discourage Hispanic girls from playing sports. Other factors, including poverty and language barriers, also keep Latina girls away from sports. The strong Latino emphasis on education as the primary pathway to success also accounts for lower numbers of female Latina athletes. But more and more in recent years, those roles have been changing, and Latino families are seeing the benefits that playing sports can have for their daughters.

Historically, there have been very few role models for Latina girls to emulate, though there have been some very successful Latina athletes. These include Lisa Fernandez, a pitcher for the U.S. national softball team, who won Olympic gold medals in 1996 and 2000; Nancy Lopez, who won forty-eight golf tournaments, including three majors; and Mary Joe Fernandez, who won two Olympic gold medals in doubles tennis. Yet the number of Latina professional athletes is few.

In recent years, many leading Latino magazines have begun to feature Latina athletes on their covers. They have sought to bring more attention to the benefits of sports for girls and to provide strong role models. *Latina*, a health, beauty, and fashion magazine, has featured profiles of U.S. women's soccer player Amy Rodriguez, professional golfer Lorena Ochoa, and Jennifer Rodriguez, a two-time bronze medalist in speed skating at the 2002 Winter Olympics and the first Cuban American to compete and medal in a Winter Olympics.

The positive effects of sports are helping to introduce more Latina girls to athletics. Parents, long seen as reluctant to encourage their daughters to join sports teams, now see sports as a way to keep their children out of trouble, get better grades, and graduate from high school. Studies have shown that Hispanic girls are at greater risk than non-Hispanic peers for teen pregnancy and obesity and are more likely to drop out of school. Sports are helping to reverse these trends.

BLACK FEMALE ATHLETES FACE MULTIPLE BARRIERS

While women in general fight for equality in sports, black female athletes face additional hurdles in their quest for equity and respect. Black female athletes face an even greater level of discrimination and negative stereotyping by fans and the media. They also face barriers to athletic involvement that include limited access to quality coaching and training; the high cost of equipment or participation; and pressure from peers to quit.

Often, fans and the media define black female athletes as too aggressive, too strong, or too athletic. Rarely are black female athletes described in more complimentary ways. An example of this is the coverage of black figure skater Debi Thomas in comparison to her main rival, German skater Katarina Witt. Thomas was consistently described as being athletic and powerful, while Witt was often described as graceful and artistic. Both women won

DESPITE THEIR MULTIPLE GRAND SLAM TITLES AND TOP WORLD RANKINGS, VENUS AND SERENA WILLIAMS HAVE NOT BEEN ABLE TO CHANGE THE PERCEPTION THAT BEAUTIFUL AND ATTRACTIVE WOMEN CAN ALSO BE STRONG AND POWERFUL.

figure skating world championships leading up the 1988 Olympic Games and both could accurately be described as being strong, athletic, powerful, graceful, elegant, and artistic. Yet Thomas never received credit for her finesse, delicacy, and aesthetic vision.

The Williams sisters, Venus and Serena, have consistently faced negativity and harsh criticism in spite of their domination of women's tennis. At the Wimbledon tournament, they were consistently scheduled to play on Court 2, not Court 1, the tennis center's larger main venue. During the 2009 Australian Open final, ESPN tennis commentator Mary Carillo criticized Serena Williams regarding her perceived commitment to the game. At the Australian Open, both sisters were left off of the tournament's list of "beautiful women of tennis." Dominating the list were slender, white European tennis players.

The Williams sisters, despite their Grand Slam titles and number one rankings, have been unable to redefine society's view of what a female athlete should look like. Black female athletes face this challenge consistently. Muscular, strong, athletic women like the Williams sisters are often on the receiving side of one recurring insult. They are told: "You look like a man."

Black women represent a very low percentage of athletes in high school and college. Less than 5 percent of all high school athletes and less than 10 percent of all college athletes are black women. They most often get involved in basketball, track and field, and other sports that are less expensive to participate in. There are very few black gymnasts, figure skaters, tennis players, and soccer players. The twenty-one-player roster of the women's 2011 U.S. World Cup team had only two Latina athletes. There were no blacks or Asians on the team.

A reason for this gap in diversity in many sports is access. Golf, tennis, and swimming do not have youth programs that serve as a pipeline to high school and college sports teams. Gymnastics, tennis, and figure skating all require extensive coaching and access to equipment not commonly found in high schools or community centers. By comparison, basketball and track and field are less expensive sports that offer easy access. In these sports, raw talent can be developed with less specialized and knowledgeable coaching. Even soccer leagues can have expensive registration fees and travel expenses that deter parents with a lower income from enrolling their children. This helps to explain why participation by young black girls is low in some sports, but high in others.

Myths and Facts

Myth

Women are naturally inferior to men in terms of strength and speed. Therefore, women aren't as good at sports as men.

Fact

Not all men are stronger, more skilled, or faster than all women. Women have greater flexibility and greater percentage of body fat, and are smaller in size compared to men. These attributes make women better at some sports than men. Marathon swimming, long-distance running, gymnastics, synchronized swimming, and horse racing are all sports that favor athletes who are flexible and smaller. For running and marathon swimming, a greater body fat percentage helps with endurance and energy consumption.

Myth

Girls cannot try out for boys' sports teams.

Fact

Girls can, in fact, try out for boys' sports team, if there is not a girls' team available in that sport. However, it's legal for a school to tell a female athlete that she cannot play in a male-dominated sport (such as football) for a legitimate non-gender-related reason, such as the athlete is too small or not strong enough, as long at that standard is fairly applied to both boys and girls.

Fact

Many stigmas still exist concerning female athletes and women's participation in sports. Society still perpetrates certain myths about female athletes designed to discourage their participation. These include:

- Girls will become more masculine if they participate in sports.
- Boys are more skillful than girls are.
- Men are stronger and more powerful than women.
- Some sports are OK for girls and women, but others aren't.
- Girls can never be as good at sports as boys.

CHAPTER 6

Juggling It All

The night before the Dubai Ladies Masters golf tournament, professional golfer Michelle Wie was up late. She wasn't thinking about her golf swing, studying the course, or worrying about the stiff competition she would face in the morning. Instead, she was working on her statistics final. Wie, a student at Stanford University, often completes homework, writes papers, and takes exams while she's traveling to professional golf tournaments around the world.

Balancing Responsibilities

Wie's life of juggling college classes and golf tournaments, coursework and travel, is a common balancing act for a student-athlete. Wie knows that once her golf career is over, she'll need something to fall back on. Her communications degree will open doors for her to continue to be involved in the world of golf (and sports in general) as a commentator or sports anchor, if she chooses. In the meantime, however, she needs to attend class, complete term

PROFESSIONAL GOLFER MICHELLE WIE BALANCES INTERNATIONAL GOLF TOURNAMENTS WITH HER ACADEMICS. A STUDENT AT STANFORD UNIVERSITY, WIE STUDIES AND COMPLETES HOMEWORK ON THE ROAD SO THAT SHE CAN EARN HER DEGREE.

papers and other assignments, study for and pass exams, and get good grades to earn her degree.

Wie's coursework has given her something else to focus on besides golf. She chose to go to college to fulfill a personal goal, but attending school has also provided her with an alternative existence when the pressures of playing professional golf get to be too much. When Wie sustained an injury that sidelined her from play, she concentrated on her studies and not on the tournaments she was missing. She also credits school with slowing down her golf career, which has helped her avoid getting burned out, a common problem for young professional athletes. Most importantly, college has given Wie, who went pro when she was just fifteen years old, a chance to enjoy all the things that ordinary twenty-somethings do and experience.

As many student-athletes will attest, playing sports, at both the high school and college levels, is a time-consuming commitment. Athletes practice five to six days a week and travel for games. They attend classes and spend much of their time off the practice field studying and working on homework assignments and class projects. They receive no extra time to complete class assignments and must participate in coursework just like everyone else. Each student-athlete is required to earn a minimum number of credits toward graduation each semester, and failing to keep up with their academics has negative implications for their athletic activities. Failing to maintain a minimum grade point average puts their athletic eligibility at risk.

Maintaining such a full schedule of athletic and academic commitments has an impact on other aspects of a student's college experience. Student-athletes often do not have time to participate in other campus activities, such as clubs or organizations. Holding down a part-time job can be difficult when free time is limited, and a full schedule of practices and games cuts into one's availability for work shifts.

Student-athletes face difficult decisions when they are offered academic opportunities that conflict with their athletic ambitions. Some athletes have given up prestigious fellowships and research grants because they would interfere with athletic pursuits by creating time-management problems and scheduling conflicts. For college athletes, commitment to the team and to their own long-term plans for a career are often at odds. Scholarships give students a chance to continue to play sports in college while providing financial support for their education. But scholarships are a contract that require students to attend all practices and games, while also maintaining a certain grade point average.

For many women, college athletics is both the high point and the conclusion of their sports careers. Since there are so few professional sports leagues for women, the vast majority of female college athletes will not play professional sports once they graduate. Their studies are important because their academic degrees will earn them a job once they complete college. Passing up a fellowship or research opportunity could hurt their long-term career goals.

While a full schedule of coursework, homework, projects, exams, practice, travel, and games can encourage the development of strong time-management skills in student-athletes, it can also lead to stress and pressure. Some college academic advisers often tell student-athletes to

ATHLETES MUST LEARN TO BALANCE THE DEMANDS OF SPORTS AND ACADEMICS, PRACTICE AND STUDY, COMPETITION AND CLASSES, WHICH CAN SOMETIMES BE AT ODDS WITH ONE ANOTHER.

choose less demanding majors if they want to play sports or if they are on a sports scholarship. While choosing a program of study with a lesser workload can help students manage their time better, this may not be the best advice for athletes on a scholarship. Many student-athletes could not afford to attend college without their scholarships. They may have been recruited to play sports for a college, but the education they receive in the classroom will have a far more enduring value—including monetary value—than the time they spend on the court or playing field.

DEPRESSION AND ATHLETICS

The pressure to balance athletic commitments with

schoolwork can lead to depression for many student-athletes. An increasing number of universities are reporting that many of their student-athletes are suffering from depression and anxiety disorders as they juggle practices, competitions, and academic demands. For some athletes, like

Division I swimmer Tiffany Clay, the stress of it all can blindside them.

Recruited to swim for the University of Tennessee, Clay found her life spinning out of control a month into her freshman year when she began suffering from migraines

EVEN DURING THE OFF-SEASON OR WHEN INJURED, STUDENT-ATHLETES MUST STAY IN SHAPE. DURING THE ATHLETIC SEASON, MANY STUDENT-ATHLETES USE THEIR FREE TIME TO GET IN EXTRA WORKOUTS TO GET A COMPETITIVE EDGE.

and had difficulty sleeping. Her coursework became challenging, and she lacked her usual drive and motivation in swim practice. Luckily for Clay, the university had a system in place to help students adjust to the stress and pressures of being an elite college athlete. When Clay's performance dropped, her coach suggested she contact a social worker at the university, who was part of a larger team of doctors, athletic trainers, sports psychologists, and academic counselors. Clay went on to become an All-American swimmer for the university.

Providing support to student-athletes is important. This is especially true for female athletes, who experience

NIKE CHALLENGES STEREOTYPING WITH AD CAMPAIGN

Nike has created buzz with an advertising campaign starring tennis player Serena Williams, skier Picabo Street, and volleyball player Gabby Reece that draws attention to the accomplishments of women in sports. "Are you looking at my titles?" asks Williams in a print ad while wearing a T-shirt that reads "Athlete" across the front. The provocative ad is meant to generate awareness of the stereotypes and inequality female athletes face, despite the accolades they have earned. The campaign was launched after radio shock jock Don Imus made racist and sexist comments about the Rutgers University women's basketball team. It also followed in the wake of interviews Nike conducted with female high school athletes, who reported that they still don't feel they are as respected as their male counterparts.

depression and anxiety at roughly twice the rate of men. Athletes are often perceived as being mentally tough and capable of solving problems. But when an athlete is spending nearly forty hours a week in practice or competition and still needs to stay on top of coursework, the stress can be overwhelming. In extreme cases, some athletes have committed suicide. Sarah Devens, a three-sport star athlete at Dartmouth College, killed herself the summer before her senior year of college. That year, Devens would have been a team captain in field hockey, ice hockey, and lacrosse.

DRUG ABUSE AMONG STUDENT-ATHLETES

College student-athletes are considered to be at a greater risk for the abuse of alcohol and other drugs, such as steroids, diet aids, ephedrine, marijuana, and psychedelic drugs, than their nonathletic peers. Social pressures and added stress from maintaining grueling academic and athletic schedules are seen as the top reasons why some student-athletes engage in drug or alcohol abuse.

Female student-athletes are not exempt from this behavior. A recent study revealed the following facts about drug and alcohol abuse by college student-athletes:

- College athletes have higher rates of alcohol abuse than their nonathletic peers, with 48 percent of female student-athletes reporting participation in binge drinking.

STUDENT-ATHLETES ARE AT A GREATER RISK FOR ABUSING SUBSTANCES SUCH AS DIET PILLS, ALCOHOL, PERFORMANCE-ENHANCING DRUGS, OR PSYCHEDELIC DRUGS DUE TO THE ADDED PRESSURES OF MEETING MULTIPLE DEMANDS ON THEIR TIME AND ENERGY AND THE WEIGHT OF EXPECTATION PLACED UPON THEM.

- Of the female student-athletes who reported being victims of sexual aggression, 68 percent reported that their assailants had been drinking at the time of the attack.

- Sixty-two percent of female collegiate gymnasts had used at least one extreme weight-loss

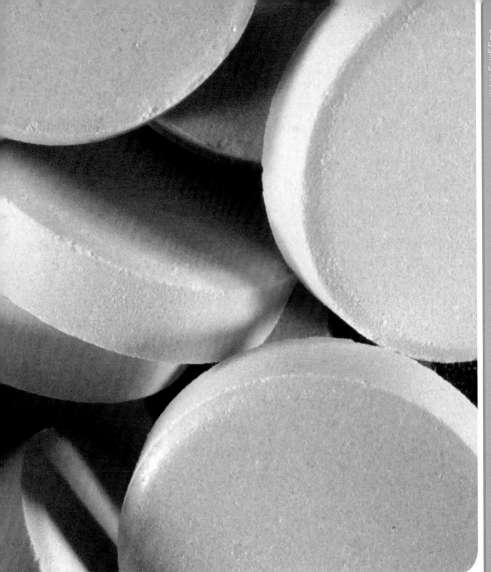

method (diet pills, etc.) at least twice a week for three or more months.

- Approximately 5 percent of college softball players use anabolic steroids.

aesthetic Relating to or dealing with the beautiful; pleasing in appearance; attractive; appreciative or responsive to the beautiful.

discrimination A prejudiced or prejudicial outlook, action, or treatment.

empowerment Having official authority or legal power; enablement.

endorsement Money earned from a product recommendation.

endurance The ability to sustain a prolonged stressful effort or activity.

equality A state in which all people have the same status, level of respect, and rights.

gender A range of characteristics used to distinguish between males and females.

heterosexism Discrimination or prejudice by heterosexuals against homosexuals.

inferior Lower in station, rank, degree, or grade.

intercollegiate Existing, carried on, or participating in activities between colleges.

legislation A law that has been enacted by a government body.

sociology The science of society, social institutions, and social relationships; the systematic study of the development, structure, interaction, and collective behavior of organized groups of human beings.

spectator A nonparticipatory observer of a sports event.

Glossary

speculation The act of meditating on or pondering a subject; the reviewing of something idly and often inconclusively.

stereotype Something conforming to a fixed or general pattern; a standardized mental picture that is held in common by members of a group and that represents an oversimplified opinion, prejudiced attitude, or uncritical judgment.

steroid Any of various chemical compounds that include numerous hormones; any of several human-made hormones that are used in medicine to help tissue grow and that are sometimes abused by athletes to increase muscle size and strength and that may have harmful effects, such as stunted growth in teens.

subjective Characteristic of or belonging to reality as it is perceived by the human mind; relating to experience or knowledge as conditioned by personal mental states or characteristics; peculiar to a particular individual; personal; modified or affected by personal views, experience, or background.

Canadian Association for the Advancement of Women
and Sport and Physical Activity (CAAWS)
N202 - 801 King Edward Avenue
Ottawa, ON K1N 6N5
Canada
(613) 562-5667
Web site: http://www.caaws.ca
CAAWS provides leadership and education and builds the
capacity to foster equitable support, diverse opportunities, and positive experiences for girls and women in
sport and physical activity.

Canadian Interuniversity Sport (CIS)
801 King Edward, Suite N205
Ottawa, ON K1N 6N5
Canada
(613) 562-5670
Web site: http://english.cis-sic.ca/landing/index
With financial assistance from the federal government,
member universities of CIS commit themselves to excellence in their sports programs, optimize their schedules,
and assign coaches to year-round programs to assist
the federal government in identifying talent, national
training centers, provision of facilities, sport research,
and testing, all with an eye on developing international
competitors.

Images of Us (IOU) Sports
4757 North 76th Street
Milwaukee, WI 53218
(414) 393-0773
Web site: http://www.iousports.org
IOU Sports provides sports education, fitness opportunities, career information, and charitable assistance to
girls and women who participate in all levels of
sports. The organization's goal is to empower girls
using sports as an avenue that instills discipline,
teamwork, and physical fitness to create well-rounded
individuals.

National Association for Girls and Women in Sport
(NAGWS)
1900 Association Drive
Reston, VA 20191
(703) 476-3453
Web site: http://www.aahperd.org/nagws
A nonprofit organization, NAGWS is the only professional educational organization devoted exclusively
to advocating for opportunities for girls and women
in sports.

National Council of Youth Sports (NCYS)
7185 Southeast Seagate Lane

Stuart, FL 34997
(772) 781-1452
Web site: http://www.ncys.org
NCYS advocates the promotion of healthy lifestyles and safe environments for stronger neighborhoods and communities while enhancing the youth sports experience in America.

Women's Sports Foundation
424 West 33rd Street, Suite 150
New York, NY 10001
(646) 845-0273
Web site: http://www.womenssportsfoundation.org
Founded in 1974 by tennis legend Billie Jean King, the Women's Sports Foundation is dedicated to advancing the lives of girls and women through sports and physical activity.

WomenSport International (WSI)
P.O. Box 743
Vashon, WA
Web site: http://www.sportsbiz.bz/womensportinternational/index.htm
WSI was formed to ensure that sports and physical activity receive the attention and priority they deserve in the lives of girls and women and to bring about positive

change for girls and women in these important areas of their lives.

Web Sites

Due to the changing nature of Internet links, Rosen Publishing has developed an online list of Web sites related to the subject of this book. This site is updated regularly. Please use this link to access the list:

http://www.rosenlinks.com/WOM/Sports

Bertine, Kathryn. *As Good as Gold: 1 Woman, 9 Sports, 10 Countries, and a 2-Year Quest to Make the Summer Olympics.* New York, NY: Random House, 2010.

Finch, Jennie. *Throw Like a Girl: How to Dream Big and Believe in Yourself.* Chicago, IL: Triumph Books, 2011.

Goldberg, Jeff, and Doris Burke. *Bird at the Buzzer: UConn, Notre Dame, and a Women's Basketball Classic.* Lincoln, NE: University of Nebraska Press, 2009.

McDonagh, Eileen, and Laura Pappano. *Playing with the Boys: Why Separate Is Not Equal in Sports.* New York, NY: Oxford University Press, 2009.

Musiker, Liz Hartman. *The Smart Girl's Guide to Sports: An Essential Handbook for Women Who Don't Know a Slam Dunk from a Grand Slam.* New York, NY: Plumer, 2008.

O'Reilly, Jean, and Susan K. Cahn, eds. *Women and Sports: A Documentary Reader.* Lebanon, NH: Northeastern University Press, 2007.

Rappoport, Ken. *Ladies First: Women Athletes Who Made a Difference.* Atlanta, GA: Peachtree Publishers, 2010.

Ross, Betsy M. *Playing Ball with the Boys: The Rise of Women in the World of Men's Sports.* Cincinnati, OH: Clerisy Press, 2010.

Samuels, Mina. *Run Like a Girl: How Strong Women Make Happy Lives.* New York, NY: Seal Press, 2011.

Sokolove, Michael. *Warrior Girls: Protecting Our Daughters Against the Injury Epidemic in Women's Sports.* New York, NY: Simon & Schuster, 2009.

Storm, Hannah. *Go Girl!: Raising Healthy, Confident, and Successful Girls Through Sports.* Chicago, IL: Sourcebooks, 2011.

Stout, Glenn. *Yes, She Can! Women's Sports Pioneers.* New York, NY: Sandpiper, 2011.

Switzer, Kathrine. *Marathon Woman: Running the Race to Revolutionize Women's Sports.* New York, NY: Da Capo Press, 2009.

Taggert, Lisa. *Women Who Win: Female Athletes on Being the Best.* New York, NY: Seal Press, 2007.

Ware, Susan. *Game, Set, Match: Billie Jean King and the Revolution in Women's Sports.* Chapel Hill, NC: The University of North Carolina Press, 2011.

Whitaker, Matthew C. *African American Icons of Sport: Triumph, Courage, and Excellence.* Boston, MA: Greenwood Press, 2008.

BIBLIOGRAPHY

Associated Press. "Michelle Wie Balancing Golf, Finals in Dubai." SI.com, December 31, 2011. Retrieved March 2012 (http://m.si.com/news/archive/archive/detail /2090544;jsessionid=3B02468E324894D53B569 5120B7FD08A.cnnsi1).

Badenhausen, Kurt. "The World's Highest-Paid Female Athletes." *Forbes*, August 1, 2011. Retrieved February 2012 (http://www.forbes.com/sites/kurtbadenhausen/ 2011/08/01/the-highest-paid-female-athletes).

Berlaige, Gai I. *Women in Baseball*. New York, NY: Praeger, 1994.

BestOnlineColleges.com. "10 Most Game Changing Female Athletes of All Time." Retrieved February 2012 (http://www.bestonlinecolleges.com/blog/2011/ 10-most-game-changing-female-athletes-of-all-time).

Brown, Ryan. "What's on TV: Not Women's Sports." Salon .com, July 13, 2010. Retrieved February 2012 (http:// www.salon.com/2010/07/13/womens_sports_ not_on_tv).

Cohen, Greta L. *Women in Sport: Issues and Controversies*. Reston, VA: American Alliance for Health, Physical Eduvation, Recreation, and Dance, 2001.

Ellis, Jena. "Biggest Milestones in U.S. Women's Sports History." SportsThenAndNow.com, July 23, 2011. Retrieved February 2012 (http://sportsthenandnow .com/2011/07/23/biggest-milestones-in-u-s-womens- sports-history).

ESPN. "New Mexico Player Banned, Apologizes."
    November 6, 2009. Retrieved February 2012
    (http://sports.espn.go.com/ncaa/news/story?id=
    4629837).

Ferguson, Doug. "Wie Has Better Balance in Her Life."
    STLToday.com, February 15, 2012. Retrieved March
    2012 (http://www.stltoday.com/sports/golf/wie-has-
    better-balance-in-her-life/article_8e21e00a-dbcc-5241-
    8f42-00f05fec0717.html).

Gardiner, Andy. "Suffering from Depression." *USA Today*,
    February 5, 2006. Retrieved March 2012 (http://
    www.usatoday.com/news/health/2006-02-05-
    womens-health-depression_x.htm).

Gavin, Mary L. "5 Reasons for Girls to Play Sports."
    KidsHealth.org, May 2011. Retrieved March 2012
    (http://kidshealth.org/teen/food_fitness/sports/
    girls_sports.html).

Gottesman, Jane. *Game Face: What Does a Female
    Athlete Look Like?* New York, NY: Random House Trade
    Paperbacks, 2003.

Griffin, Pat. *Strong Women, Deep Closets: Lesbians and
    Homophobia in Sport*. Champaign, IL: Human Kinetics,
    1998.

Harper, Sheri Fresonke. "Natalie Gulbis, the LPGA, and
    the Golfer as Sex Debate." Yahoo!Voices, April 3,
    2008. Retrieved March 2012 (http://voices.yahoo.
    com/natalie-gulbis-lpga-golfer-1346365.html).

Hellmich, Nanci. "Athletes' Hunger to Win Fuels Eating Disorders." *USA Today*, February 5, 2006. Retrieved February 2012 (http://www.usatoday.com/news/health/2006-02-05-women-health-cover_x.htm).

Joplin, Linda. "Twenty-Five Years After Title IX: Women Gain in Steps, No Leaps." NOW.org. Retrieved February 2012 (http://www.now.org/nnt/05-97/titleix.html).

Kane, Mary Jo. "Sex Sells Sex, Not Women's Sports." *Pittsburgh Post-Gazette*, August 28, 2011. Retrieved February 2012 (http://www.post-gazette.com/pg/11240/1170120-109-0.stm?cmpid=newspanel6).

Lesko, Jean. "AAGPBL League History." AAGPBL.org. Retrieved February 2012 (http://www.aagpbl.org/index.cfm/pages/league/12/league-history).

McDonagh, Eileen, and Laura Pappano. *Playing with the Boys: Why Separate Is Not Equal in Sports*. New York, NY: Oxford University Press, 2009.

NCAA. "Balancing Time Demands." Retrieved March 2012 (http://www.ncaa.org/wps/wcm/connect/public/NCAA/Student-Athlete+Experience/Student-Athlete+Well+Being/Life+balance).

New York Times. "Title IX Back on Track." April 20, 2010. Retrieved March 2012 (http://www.nytimes.com/2010/04/21/opinion/21wed3.html).

NielsenWire. "Danica Drives Racing Ratings and Buzz."
    February 24, 2012. Retrieved March 2012 (http://
    blog.nielsen.com/nielsenwire/media_entertainment/
    danica-drives-racing-ratings-and-buzz/?utm_source=
    feedburner&utm_medium=feed&utm_campaign=Feed%
    3A+NielsenWire+(Nielsen+Wire)).

Pappano, Laura, and Eileen McDonagh. "Women and
    Men in Sports: Separate But Not Equal." *Christian
    Science Monitor*, January 31, 2008. Retrieved
    February 2012 (http://www.csmonitor.com/
    Commentary/Opinion/2008/0131/p09s01-
    coop.html).

Plummer, William. "Dying for a Medal." *People*, August
    22, 1994. Retrieved January 27, 2012 (http://www
    .people.com/people/archive/article/0,,20103704,
    00.html).

Rotondi, Jessica Pearce. "Danica Patrick and the 'Danica
    Effect.'" *Huffington Post*, February 27, 2012. Retrieved
    March 2012 (http://www.huffingtonpost.com/jessica-
    pearce-rotondi/danica-patrick-danica-effect_b_
    1305443.html).

Schwartz, Larry. "Martina Was Alone on Top." ESPN.
    Retrieved March 2012 (http://espn.go.com/
    sportscentury/features/00016378.html).

Shipley, Amy. "Jones Pleads Guilty, Admits Using Steroids."
    Washington Post, October 6, 2007. Retrieved

February 2012 (http://www.washingtonpost
.com/wp-dyn/content/story/2007/10/05/
ST2007100502097.html?sid=ST2007100502097).

Stenson, Jacqueline. "Kids on Steroids Willing to Risk It All
for Success." MSNBC, March 3, 2008. Retrieved
February 2012 (http://www.msnbc.msn.com/
id/22984780/ns/health-childrens_health/t/kids-
steroids-willing-risk-it-all-success/#.TO5G8szs2xE).

Sylwester, MaryJo. "Culture, Family Play Role in Sports for
Latina Girls." USA Today, March 29, 2005. Retrieved
February 2012 (http://www.usatoday.com/
sports/2005-03-28-hispanic-tradition_x.htm).

Tapia, Andres. "U.S. Women's Soccer: Not Quite
America's Team." New America Media, July 27,
2011. Retrieved March 2012 (http://newamerica
media.org/2011/07/us-womens-soccer-not-quite-
americas-team.php).

USA Today. "Nike Serves Up New Ads Supporting
Women." August 27, 2007. Retrieved March 2012
(http://www.usatoday.com/money/advertising/
adtrack/2007-08-26-ad-track-williams_N.htm).

Williams, Lena. "Hispanic Female Athletes Few and Far
Between." Puerto Rico Herald, November 6, 2002.
Retrieved March 2012 (http://www.puertorico-herald.
org/issues/2002/vol6n46/HispFemaleAthlet-en.html).

Women's Sports Foundation. "Mythbusting: What Every
Female Athlete Should Know." Retrieved March 2012

(http://www.womenssportsfoundation.org/en/
sitecore/content/home/athletes/for-athletes/know-
your-rights/athlete-resources/mythbusting-what-every-
female-athlete-should-know.aspx).

Woods, Jewel. "Venus and Serena Williams: Ousted
by Racism." Huffington Post, February 27, 2009.
Retrieved March 2012 (http://www.huffingtonpost.
com/jewel-woods/venus-and-serena-williams_b_
169927.html).

About the Author

Laura La Bella is a lifelong runner who recently took up cycling and is mastering the art of kayaking. She is a writer who lives, works, paddles, and runs in and around Rochester, New York.

Photo Credits

Designer: Nicole Russo; Photo Researcher: Karen Huang